praise for

# GETTING N

*If you're looking for an actual roadmap to getting noticed online instead of continuing to waste your time on fleeting motivational fluff, this should be your next read.*

- Elizabeth Bienas (VP of Operations + Business Owner)

*Lindsay brings her no nonsense, no fluff to the pages by giving you smart, straightforward, and entertaining advice on all things social media. A must read for any boss lady who wants to step up their online presence. This book is everything.*

- Carrie Hoener (Mom of 3 + Business Owner)

*Getting Noticed has not only helped me, but will help my team understand how to expand their reach in a growing and changing social media driven world.*

- Janell Vonigas (Mom of 3 + Business Owner)

*Getting Noticed in a must-read for every entrepreneur looking to improve and maximize their digital reach. You don't want to miss your opportunity. Whether you are just starting out or have been in the game for years, it's never too late to do it right!*

- Kelly Anderson-Block (Event Director, Twin Mom + Business Owner)

*If you're looking to increase your knowledge in social media to further your business, this is the book. Lindsay has made this information easy to understand and apply to your business so that you can take your business to the next level. If you can only get one book about social media, this is the one.*

- Melissa Koehler (Photographer, Mom of 3 + Business Owner)

# GETTING NOTICED

A No-Nonsense Guide to Standing Out
and Selling More for Momtrepreneurs
Who 'Ain't Got Time for That'

Lindsay Teague Moreno

Book art design, illustrations, and cover design by Jennifer Lake at LTM Consulting, LLC in collaboration with Lindsay Teague Moreno.

ISBN

Second Edition: July 2017

For my girls, Boston, Teagan & Kennedy.

Made possible by their daddy who brings me coffee to coax me out of bed in the morning, without which this book would never have been finished because, sleep. Tomorrow, coffee is on me, M. I love you.

# TABLE OF CONTENTS

# INTRODUCTION

# Introduction

·

Can I be super real with you right off the bat? I've read a business book or two or ten. I've also purchased the "secret to social media" eBooks that pop up every other month online. Maybe this will be the one with real, usable content, I think. What I've found is that most of these books are missing that part between introducing what social media is and how to actually implement positive change in the way we present ourselves, our business, and connect with customers online. It's book after book, PDF after PDF, of "change everything you're doing on social media and just be me, simple as that." Ummmm, nope. That's just not a thing. Ladies, we're in a unique place in the market. We need information, and we need it fast. It needs to be pointed, and it actually needs to help us make our businesses more successful. We don't have time for fluff, y'all. There's far less time in the day than items on our to-do list, even Santa is jealous of our list at this point. Kids are screaming at us because we gave them Drumsticks and string cheese for lunch (again), and they're ready for a snack approximately 2.3 seconds after finishing their meal, amiright? We actually have to switch the laundry that's gone through 13 wash cycles into the dryer at some point so we can put off folding it and putting it away. Trust me, I know the game because I live the hardcore mom life. How are we supposed to juggle our roles as stay-at-home moms and entrepreneurs when our time is filled up with books, events, and online courses that end up leaving us with some temporary warm fuzzies but no content to actually help us build a business? Ain't nobody got time for that. I know you're busy and I know your time is precious. I promise to try to give you some real, tangible and usable content to help you step up your game and get more eyes on your business.

I've been an entrepreneur in some capacity since I was 25. Entrepreneurship is in my blood. In 2013, I started a business from nothing that grew into a team of over 300,000 people producing over $15,000,000 each month in just three years. One year in, my husband started working with me and we were able to expand our business into multiple new ventures. I always thought that the money would be the most rewarding part of seeing that kind of success because, hello, dolla dolla bills, y'all. Also, I thought people who said, "It's not about the money,

money can't buy happiness" were complete liars. *Sure, of course it's not, rich dude. Say that again while not laughing into your ascot because I'd be real happy if this car payment didn't exist.* I'm eating my piece of humble pie though, because the money I've made has purchased the absolute freedom to say yes to pretty much anything. It's not the first class flights and fancy handbags that I value the most. The best part is the feeling of freedom. Nobody owns us; not our time, not our paychecks, not our free time, not our workday. We are the boss around here. Don't let anybody tell you being your own boss isn't worth every bit of the hustle. Plus, I love the people I have come to know through my businesses. They have become a part of me and an integral part of my story. I have had others give so selflessly to me, not only their time, energy, and commitment to our business, but also actual physical gifts of love, a card, a hand-written note, a bouquet of flowers, a hand-made piece of art, a token of love from their home town. I've saved them all because they're physical representations of their love for me you can't buy that.

With the freedom to be able to either quit working and win the world record for most potato chips consumed in a single day, or work to help others do what I have been blessed to be able to do, I choose work. I need work. I didn't start my business because I wanted to be a millionaire. I started it because I wanted to connect with other moms who were feeling like there had to be more to life than diapers, drop-off lines in the perfect Lululemon workout outfit, and tricking your kids into eating food... literally any piece of food.

This is my time to open the playbook of what I've learned over the years and to help others do so much more than what I've been able to do. This isn't about helping you become me. I want to help you become the you that people really, really like. The world of female entrepreneurship has shown me so much love over the past three years, it's your turn to feel the love. I hope you feel that love and real desire for your success throughout this book as you make your way through each of the sections. Simply getting noticed is such an important part of entrepreneurial success in our fast-paced, online-based world. Let's find a way to do just that, shall we? Come on, I'll hold your hand and tell you what I know in the simplest and fastest way I can. I know you can do this. Let's get some eyes on your product because we need it, we just don't know it yet.


XOXO,

LTM

# I

# REAL HUSTLE ISN'T SEXY

## PART ONE

# Real Hustle Isn't Sexy

What I'm about to ask of you in this book is going to take a lot of work and a lot of hustle, and we're only just tackling the social media portion of your business. It's not going to be easy and most people won't be willing to do what they need to do to succeed. You're not one of those people, though. This is your dream and you're prepared to fight for it. I see you.

Let's talk about real hustle, though. I'm talking about the not sexy part. Too many times when people hear the success story -- the "I came from the bottom and now I'm here" story -- they only see the sexy part. That's the fame, the pats on the back, the smiles, the stages, the lights, the money, the toys, the payoff, etc. What's missing in that equation are a bunch of hours (if you're to believe Malcom Gladwell, at least 10,000 hours) of the opposite of glamorous; I'm talking about downright gritty.

You guys, there is nothing, and I mean it, nothing sexy about the grind, even if social media tries to sex it up. The everyday in-and-out is hard. I'm not even really sure how else to say it. There's not a word to describe it; it's the closest thing to impossible I can think of. The payoff? That's the sexy part, but you're going to have to bet big on the results to make it through the grind. Is your dream big enough to be worth it? I'll tell you right now, for many of us, it's not. We're going to need to go bigger.

In my case, when I first started my business, my husband and I agreed on the amount of time I was going to put into building it because I wanted my payout faster. He allowed me to work one hundred-hour workweeks when I needed to. That will not be the case for most people because, honestly, most people are not going to be able to pull that off. It's not a flaw, it's not a knock on what you do; it's just reality. Most people will not wake up at 7:30 and work without ceasing until 2:00 a.m. because they have other obligations and they care about their kids eating food and getting picked up from school. Some people might, but I'm here to tell you that the more you put in, the more you get out. I'm not saying that working that much is the right thing or a requirement. I let absolutely everything else I loved go during those years when I was building my business.

Only you can make the choice on what you're willing to put in. It's also your choice how much effort you put into each day, being honest about the quality of the hours you're putting in. Are you being intentional with the hours you have to give? Because if you're just messing around on the internet and calling it work, you're fooling yourself. If you're telling people you're an entrepreneur and you're not sacrificing other things, you're fooling yourself. If you expect to have an output of 100% and you're only willing to put in an input of 30%, you're fooling yourself.

But don't forget that success doesn't come without a cost. It takes sacrifice and compromise and determination and grit.

You want to know what my gritty looks like?

It's a house that's a wreck, like so bad you're embarrassed to look at it yourself. It's an amount of mom guilt that could crush a soul. It's getting fatter. It's staring at a computer so long your eyes burn. It's losing massive amounts of sleep. It's fights with your spouse over priorities. It's pressure beyond what you ever thought you were capable of. It's wearing the same pair of underwear two days in a row. It's constant noise in your head even after your kids go to bed. It's the feeling that you don't know what you're doing...ever. It's being put down and labeled for your vision. It's taking huge risks and losing. It's putting your name on the line over and over and over. It's taking a lot of blame. It's making choices that could affect and hurt your business if you're wrong. It's standing up for what you believe is the

**IF YOU EXPECT TO HAVE AN OUTPUT OF 100% and you're only willing to put in AN INPUT OF 30% you're fooling yourself**

right thing when it's not popular. It's being the bad guy. It's being hated. It's impossibly long hours. It's exhaustion to the point of tears. It's rage on some days. It's mostly thankless. It can be horribly lonely at times. It's not sexy.

You get the point.

You will get out what you put in. Scratch that. That's not true. Sometimes, you'll get out less than you put in. Sometimes, though, you'll get that break in the clouds and your work starts to pay off and you start to hear those angels sing. Something YOU did makes a difference in other people's lives and on that day, you'll feel indescribable happiness. You'll get those butterflies in your stomach. You'll be so excited you actually dance. You'll have perma-smile. If you're doing it right, you'll love the grind. It's not sexy and it's not easy, but you will love doing it and you'll be willing to give up what you need to in order to reach your goals and dreams.

For most of us, let's just be honest here (and not get defensive)...we need to step up our game. If we're going to be comparing our input to other people's output, we need to get our butts in gear. I'm not saying that because I expect you to be a workhorse. That's not possible and I don't even think it's healthy. We need to put in good, quality hours. We need to figure out what we can give up. We need to be really clear about why we're doing this. We need to pinpoint what derails us. We need to be honest about the amount of work we're willing to put in and then we need to go and JUST DO IT.

Just do it.

Don't make excuses. Don't wait for someone else to motivate you. Don't blame other people for your lack of growth. Just work. That's all. Just go to work. If you aren't sure what to do, read. If you don't have a needed skill, learn it.

JUST DO IT.

Stop with the excuses. Stop telling yourself lies that you're going to be able to have this perfect, balanced life while you grind out a winning business. No, you won't. I don't know a person alive who has started a ground-up business and did it in a sexy way. Let's get real with ourselves. Most of us are not busting our butts every day. We're not. That's okay. Let's be real about it and let's also be real about the ROI (return on investment) we can expect from the amount we're putting in each day.

Start here and honestly answer these fill-in-the-blank questions:

*I'm running this business because:* _____

_____

_____

_____

_____

*Right now, I'm giving* _____ *% of real, solid, uninterrupted effort to my business.*

*I want to be giving* _____ *%.*

*In order to make these two numbers match, I need to:* _____

_____

_____

_____

_____

Now go do what needs to be done. Do it for you. Do it for your family. Connect with why you started this in the first place and put your effort into it. Set your boundaries and stick to them. I don't regret the effort I put into creating a healthy, sustainable business even though it took sacrifice. I don't believe you will be either. Like I said before, the world needs your product or service. We need your perspective. We need you. We're depending on you to want this thing so much you refuse to fail at it.

# 2

# THE
# GROUNDWORK

**PART TWO:**

# The Groundwork

Let's just cut to the chase. Doing prep work of any kind is not my strong suit. I'm not the person that lays out my kids' clothes the night before and gets dinners planned a week in advance, but my life would be easier if I did and I know it. I've learned the hard way how important prep work is when it comes to creating and posting content that I want my audience to read. We're going to have to do some important work before we start posting on social media.

When it comes to creating the best content, the preparation is what gives your posts magic. You need to know what you want to say, how you plan to say it, and what it will look like on various social media outlets before you just haphazardly put something "out

WHEN IT COMES TO CREATING

## THE BEST CONTENT

### THE PREPARATION

is what gives your posts

*magic*

9

there" for the world to see. Now, before you think this is an impossible expectation, please understand, I'm a "shortest distance between two points" kind of girl. If it takes an average of 15 minutes to complete a task, I'm looking for a way to cut that down by at least half. In my head, preparation just makes a task longer. Why spend precious moments crafting and planning when there is so much to get done? No thank you. Me and laying groundwork are not friends. Planning is not my favorite part of any undertaking because I'm anxious for the work, not the talking about the work.

Earlier this year I wrote a book proposal which required the most prep work I've ever done in my life — ever. But I did it because I was told by an expert that I should write a proposal before I actually begin to write the book itself. It's my job to learn from someone who has gone before me, and I wanted to do this thing right the first time. Sometimes, I can do what I'm told (shhh, don't tell my husband!). The prep work was long and arduous and often frustrating. I could have trained for an Iron Man Triathlon in the time it took to complete each section but I wouldn't do that because, running. The point is, I would have been a disorganized mess if the proposal hadn't come before the actual book because I need a guide for this process.

My husband, Michael, on the other hand, is really disciplined at doing all of the prep work before he starts a project. Let's take, for example, our IKEA furniture purchase of 2012, a day that shall live in infamy.

I think it takes him forever to finish a project but when he finishes, it's usually right. I just start nailing things together and don't realize until the end I'm missing an entire chair leg. (Nobody should ever hire me to put together IKEA furniture. It ain't pretty.) I've had to learn (over and over again) that preparation makes me more efficient in the long run, rather than seeing it as a nuisance that slows me down. If you're like Michael, your little brain is probably firing off massive amounts of dopamine at the thought of organizing things and putting everything together before starting. The prep work you do will make you better in the long run.

So before you post on Instagram, before you update your Facebook feed or Pinterest page, I'm going to ask you to consider some questions that can be hard to answer. They may take some time and introspection about what you really want and the point of your business, but I promise you it will make your social media posts more cohesive. If you do this preparation work, your posts will get more views, more interaction, and they'll be more purposeful than throwing content at the wall and hoping it sticks. By contrast, I want you to nail content to the wall and make it stick.

If you want people to want what you have to offer, you first need to understand it yourself. As corporate as it sounds, you need a mission and vision statement. These two things will serve as the basis for everything you do, say, post, and put into the world about your business. You'll also need to spend time defining your target market and putting on paper who your audience is. You will come away knowing precisely who it is that will buy your product so you know exactly how to talk to them. Then we'll talk about your brand and what makes you different than your competition. We will hone in on your unique selling proposition and how to use that to attract attention from all the right people in all the right ways.

## Craft Your Mission + Vision Statements

It might seem cliché to ask you to create a mission statement and a vision statement for your business. I mean, that's what big businesses do and what does it even really do for them? The best time to create a mission and vision for your company or product is right at the beginning when it's just you and your big dreams for your little company. Trust me, once things get complicated and you've got orders coming out of your ears, you're going to be glad for the mission and vision to keep you on track and staying consistent when you have decisions to make and employees to hire. You may not be able to see it now, but not so far off in your distant future, you're going big, my friend. You're not settling for an average at-home business, you're an entrepreneur. It's time to give your business the respect it deserves. It's time to treat your business like a legit, valid, and valuable venture.

So what, you might be asking yourself, is the difference between a mission and a vision statement? I'm so glad you asked!

Though similar, there are some important differences between the two statements, and you'll need both for your business no matter how big, small, narrow, or broad your company is now or may become. A mission statement answers the fundamental questions about what your company does and who you do it for. A vision statement, by contrast, shows a big picture of what the company will become in the future. Think of the mission in terms of TODAY and the vision in terms of TOMORROW; the mission informs and the vision inspires. What is your company on a mission to do? Write that in the mission statement. What is your vision for the future of your company? Write that in the vision statement.

Before I throw out some examples from amazing companies for you to look at, I want you to expand your ideas of what a vision and a mission need to be. One thing they do not need to be is bland. Resist boring corporate jargon, who is a fan of that? Mission and vision statements should leave out complicated words and ideas altogether. Both get a bad rap because we put them in a tiny, ordinary, craft-colored box with too many words. Instead, let your mission and vision be as colorful, authentic, and full of life as your product or service is in your dreams. Destroy

ET YOUR MISSION AND VISION

*be as colorful,*

**AUTHENTIC,**

*and full of life*

ιs your product or service

**N YOUR DREAMS**

the box you think your mission and vision need to fit into, and create statements with originality, purpose, and flavor. Here are some amazing mission and vision statement examples from some of my favorite out-of-the-box companies.

**Warby Parker** (https://www.warbyparker.com)

Mission Statement: "Warby Parker was founded with a rebellious spirit and a lofty objective: to offer designer eyewear at a revolutionary price, while leading the way for socially conscious businesses."

Vision Statement: "We believe that buying glasses should be easy and fun. It should leave you happy and good-looking, with money in your pocket."

Why I love it: Warby-Parker is one of my favorite examples of quality mission and vision statements, because they believe in what I believe in — challenging the status quo. Your mission and vision should help others come alongside your business in shared belief. When I see everything Warby Parker stands for, I think to myself, "Warby Parker and I believe the same thing! I'll buy my glasses from them because we're similar and I like what they stand for." Notice that their mission statement says what they do right now. "Was founded on" is a past tense statement and the word choice is intended to intentionally connect with a younger audience. Did someone say rebellious and revolutionary in one sentence? Take my money. Their vision points decision makers in the direction they should be going. Any person that works at Warby Parker can now look at each decision though the vision lens and have a better understanding of what will be a yes and what will be a no.

**Kate Spade New York** (www.katespadeandcompany.com/)

Mission Statement: "Kate Spade New York draws women into a world that's culturally curious, intellectually alive, and glowing with irresistible allure. There are stories to capture the imagination and dramas to unfold. Kate Spade New York encourages women to star in their own lives. To be courageous. To indulge their many passions. To tune out the noise of fashion fads and mediocrity in all its forms. Kate Spade is the brand that helps women express their own personal style with incandescent charm and a dash of rebellion."

Vision Statement: "Crisp color, graphic prints and playful sophistication are the hallmarks of Kate Spade New York. From handbags and clothing to jewelry, fashion accessories, fragrance, eyewear, shoes, swimwear, home decor, desk accessories, stationery, tabletop and gifts, our exuberant approach to the everyday encourages personal style with a dash of incandescent charm. We call it living colorfully."

Why I love it: Kate Spade New York lays it all out for you. I can almost imagine what their product might look like or what the woman who buys the product might look like without ever seeing it/her. One thing that I love about Kate Spade is that her products are everything that she describes. One look at one of her pieces and you already know it's hers. She's brand consistent in the best way, probably because she went to town on the vision and mission of her company.

**Google** (www.google.com)

Mission Statement: "To organize the world's information and make it universally accessible and useful."

Vision Statement: "To provide access to the world's information in one click."

Why I love it: Google doesn't mince words. The company with the most information at its disposal isn't wasting your time explaining how much they make or how huge they are. They're simply telling you what they do now and what they want to be in the future. One thing I love about Google is that their unofficial motto is to "avoid being evil." That makes me smile. You can find that statement connected to their name all over the internet. Just Google it and see — see what I did there?

*#PROTIP: Richard Branson, who certainly knows a thing or two about successful business, advises that you stick to the twitter 140-character rule when it comes to your mission. Don't over-explain it. Get in, say what you mean, and get out.*

## Define Your Target Market

Where did your product idea or vision come from? Like most brilliant ideas, it probably came from a problem you encountered at one time, or because something was missing in your life and you thought, "I bet I can do that." Before long, you probably realized that your product might be what's missing in someone else's life, too. For my business, the formation of my team and subsequent businesses were born out of a desire to connect with like-minded women who wanted to approach entrepreneurship in a totally new way. I created my team as a place to belong because I didn't belong anywhere else. I've always been "different." I don't like regular mom stuff. I've never been the cool kid. I don't think like most women. I tend to go right when everyone else goes left, and sometimes that makes me feel lonely. I knew that if I felt a need to be something more than just a mom, there were probably other women who felt the same. In order for me to attract those women, I had to define my target market. The great news is that my target market is me! I already have all the answers about my customer because I am her. You might find yourself in the same situation, especially if your product or service was something you created to meet your own need.

If you want to attract others to your brand, product, or service, you're going to have to know who they are first. When you can paint the complete picture of the person who will be your consumer, you'll have an easier time talking to them and connecting with them. So who is your customer? Here are a few questions to help you build the picture of your customer. Answer these questions very specifically.

Are they men or women?

How old are they?

Where do they live?

How many kids do they have?

Are they married?

How much money do they make?

What do they like to do in their free time?

What do they do during their day?

What kind of things are they interested in?

What kind of lifestyle do they live?

What are their hobbies?

What is holding them back?

What are they afraid of?

What injustice affects them the most?

Remember that being specific when it comes to your target market is a good thing. It doesn't mean you won't attract anyone outside of that core audience, it just means you understand who you're connecting with. Everything you put out on the web when it comes to your company, product, or service will have this person in mind. You're likely going to get a lot of amazing customers who are "outliers," meaning outside of your target market, but that doesn't mean you should direct your posts to every kind of person who might be following you on social media. You aim for the core. I see so many amazing businesses with great potential start trying to be everything for everyone; which, let's be honest, is just impossible. They lose out on making loyal connections with their target market because they are spending so much time trying to attract customers who are not in their demographic in the first place. Do your business a favor (and save yourself some energy) and narrow down a target audience.

## The Brand of YOU

This might well be the most important part of creating content that gets noticed — you. You are by far the most important part.

Not who you want to be.

Not who you think you need to be.

Not the version of yourself you think people want to see.

Just you.

You're enough just as you are.

You might not believe it right now, that's okay. I hope you do by the end of this little book. You are the secret to your success. Here's a numbered list of reasons you should believe me:

1. You have a unique set of talents, abilities, skills, connections, experiences, and ideas that no other person on the planet can replicate.

Only you. All you need to do is figure out how to use them together to create some magic.

2. You know your product or service better than anyone on the planet because it came from you. It originated in your unique, brilliant brain. If there's something to sell, you are the woman for the job because you know what you do better than anyone else.

3. The people that are following you are doing so for a reason. Either they know you from the past or they chose to know you now. Either way, you have something they were attracted to. You're the common denominator there.

4. When people can see that you (not your product) have something in common with them, they start to believe, rightfully so, that what you like, they also like. For example, if I find out someone else likes scrapbooking like I do, I make the jump that we like all kinds of the same things. So when they tell me they love their product that they created, it's easy for me to say, "Well, we like similar things, so I will probably like this product, too." Commonality creates trust and trust sells products.

5. Science tells us that human beings connect through stories and emotions (even if, like me, you're uncomfortable with all the feels). That means when Seth Godin wrote, "People don't buy goods and services, they buy relations, stories, and magic," he was right. It's science. When Simon Sinek said in his famous TED talk, "People don't buy what you do, they buy why you do it," he was right because, science. Our buying

decisions are made in the limbic brain where our feelings are stored. Stories create feelings. Ever cried at a movie, while reading a book, or at moving Facebook post? I rest my case. It's not the product that sells. It's you. All along, you were selling yourself and you just might not have known it. Case in point, I have a house full of things I'll never use because I was inspired by a person to buy their product simply because I liked them. I believed what they believe. I saw myself in them. I saw something in their life that I wanted for my own. We all do it. Don't lie, you do it, too. Want proof? Etsy — the place where my paycheck goes to die and where the best storytellers win.

All of this is the reason that I tell people they need to be working way harder on the brand of themselves than the brand of the product they're selling. Your product can't suck, let's say that out front. But simply focusing on the product and what you have to offer people as far as your good or service is concerned, only goes so far to convince people to click "buy." You want people to notice what you post? You need to be working harder on selling the brand of you.

Tell more stories. Everything you write should be in story form, friends.

Be who you are.

Write like you speak.

Inspire and entertain people.

Let people into your world.

Connect with others by starting conversations with them.

Be vulnerable.

Let people see the good and the bad.

Show them you're a real person.

Let them cheer you on.

Here's the hardest one: be willing to let people not like you and talk about you online. Be willing to let them rip apart the thing you've put so much of your heart, soul, time, and energy into creating. Let them do it because it's worth it. #HatersGonnaHate

The bottom line is, if you want your stuff to be noticed, it needs to be authentic. That means it needs to come from you because people don't buy from those they don't trust. It's the reason that online reviews exist. We want a shortcut to answer the question, "Can we trust them with our money?" Show people they can trust you by being who you really are —the quirky, silly, a little insane, creative, big-hearted person that comes along with the product you sell. Make your personality work for you. Don't be afraid. It works. I've seen it work thousands of times. There isn't a person on the planet that can replicate what you're about to do, it's just up to you to do it.

# CREATING CONTENT WITH INTENTION

# PART THREE:

# Creating Content with Intention

This is the part of the book where we start getting into the nuts and bolts of how to get noticed. At this time, you should have a pretty good grasp on why you're doing what you're doing and what your intentions are for your product or service. You'll need to fall back on all of that as we start to actually craft content to present to potential customers. In this section, we're going to learn how to organize, plan, write, and schedule your posts. I hear a lot of people say they just don't know what to write on every single day. Fear not, you're going to have topics coming out of your ears after you understand this. One thing that you should understand before we move forward is that your content is going to take a lot of time. You'll have to schedule it into your day. If you're used to just posting on a whim when you have a few minutes, you're about to make some drastic changes to the way you do business. Your social media is a business tool, not just a way to tell your story. If you're smart, you'll use it as both, but you'll need to be strategic about it. That means spending more time preparing — there's that nasty word again.

**your social media IS A BUSINESS TOO *not just a way* TO TELL YOUR STORY**

### Organize

I find the posts that get a lot of traffic, be it on a blog or on social media, are the posts where you can entertain, inspire or simply teach people something new. I love when I can learn a new tip or tidbit from an Instagram post as I'm scrolling through. I stop for them. Have you ever noticed what you stop for on social media? It's likely that the person writing the post organized the content beforehand in order to make sure you saw it on that day. If you've followed me on social media for even a day, you've likely figured out that organization isn't something I was born to love. While I have to have a clean desk to work, keeping it that way is a challenge. When I say challenge, I really mean that my six-year-old picks up better than I do. I'm lucky to have a husband because a good housewife I am not. I have to remind Michael that I'm good at other things, one of those things being business. See? It works.

When it comes to social media and making the most of my efforts online, organization is key. You simply cannot just throw things "out there" without thought and effort and hope they make it. You need to be strategic about it. I lead a Facebook group in which I am very intentional about where and when and what I post. The point of the group is to teach leadership and entrepreneurship based on what I've learned and others have taken the time to teach me. I make sure to consistently show up and make myself available to the people in the group. Here are a few of the things I do to gather ideas and begin to organize the content that I will eventually share. You should be able to use this information to help you organize both social media posts and blog content.

Step 1: Make a secret Pinterest board. I find Pinterest is such an easy way to consolidate information from any place on the internet where I can access it from virtually anywhere. You can call it anything you want. "CONTENT IDEAS" comes to mind, but if you want to call it "Susan" that's fine, too. Your board, your choice, I don't judge.

Step 2: Make a new folder in the photos app on your phone. On the iPhone, click photos>albums>+ and then name the album whatever will work for you. If you're a momtrepreneur on the move like me, you have a lot of balls in the air at one time and you work a lot from your phone. This is a great way to screen shot content that you see around the internet that can't be pinned (hello, Insta and Snapchat and Facebook). I call my folder "QUOTES + CONTENT" because I'm basically a genius.

Step 3: Take some time each day to observe what your target market cares about. You can do this through pretty much any internet forum. Read blogs, scan Facebook, scroll Instagram, peruse Pinterest, read through Facebook groups you're a part of.

What are they saying?

What are they talking about?

What is frustrating them?

What needs do they have?

What is exciting them?

What's trending right now?

What are you seeing that other people are doing really well?

How can you incorporate their lessons into your own brand?

I generally do this in the mornings because it's not an activity that takes a whole lot of concentration and thinking. Some of us (ah-hem) are not at our best in the morning times. When Michael tells my girls "don't poke the bear" before 9:00 a.m., it's because I'm likely to rip your face clean off if you ask me to do anything before coffee hits my side table. I'm not proud.

Step 4: As you're observing, if you come across something that catches your eye that you think you could use to inspire content, put it either in your secret Pinterest board or screen shot it and put it in your phone folder. You might not write on it today, but you certainly could use it in the future when the "what can I write about today" question pops up.

Step 5: Repeat steps 4 & 5 at least a couple of times a week. I do it daily. Things change so fast. What you think is relevant today may not be in a month or two, so be consistent on this activity.

Step 6: Move on to the planning phase.

## Plan

Now that you have an abundance of content to craft into something your customers will want to read and engage with, it's time to move into the planning phase. In this phase you're going to get out a calendar and actually plan out your content. I find it's really helpful to stick to one topic a few days in a row for a couple of reasons. First, it can be good for people to get information in smaller chunks as far as retention goes. You're going to learn later the importance of keeping things simple, short, and sweet; especially if you're talking about a post on Instagram or Facebook. When you break up what would normally be one post into smaller pieces, people are not only more likely to read what you write, but they're also more likely to retain the information. Second, your posts will get put into different people's feeds based on the algorithm of the platform you're using. By posting a few different times about the same thing, you'll have a better chance of more people seeing the content you're trying to serve up.

For my business blog, I choose one day each month to create a theme or topic, and I have contributing writers submit posts about that certain topic from different viewpoints. Inviting other writers to share on your blog is a great way to "give back" to your community of loyal followers by sharing your platform with them. I also post motivational quotes or mini-lessons about that topic on social media to help drive home the point or pique people's interest. This approach works when your service is education but may not work as well if you have a product you're trying to promote. Consider shorter stints on a certain topic for a product. Also, you could entertain the possibility

**INVITING OTHER WRITERS TO SHARE ON YOUR BLOG is a great way to GIVE BACK TO YOUR COMMUNITY**

of doing something consistently during different days of the week. For example, every Monday, you know that moms are likely trying to recover from the weekend at home with their kids. If your target market is moms, you could do a peek into your real life every Monday so other mom's know they're not alone. Call it something catchy and very you, like "Momtrepreneur Monday" and try to be consistent about posting. People need consistency to be on the lookout for what you post, especially if they know they're going to like the content. The trick is to make sure you plan out and write down what you need to post and when you're going to do it before you move onto the writing and scheduling portion.

## Write

For me, this is the most fun part because it means actually working and doing something rather than just planning on working one day in the near future. The reason I work at all is because I have this innate need to use my brain for something of substance and purpose each day. If I don't, I notice my mood shifts (in the wrong direction), and I'll start to either pick fights or make bad choices to give my brain something to do. I'm basically the opposite of Jack from the movie, The Shining. "All play and no work, makes Lindsay a dull girl." I know this makes me weird. I embrace the weird. Moving on.

My business grew 100% from social media over the last three years and I've learned the hard way what to do and what not to do. We're going to talk a lot more about how to write and what you should actually say, but here I want to give you a few #ProTips based on what I've learned in my years of using social media to not only grow a following but also to sell a product.

Tip #1: Create content based on what is inspiring you or what you learned in your online browsing. This may require you to do some research and read a little about your topic of choice, especially if you want to give some tips or educate your audience. I often like to see what's already written out there to make sure I'm being original in what I'm saying. I want to make sure I'm also adding value and not just regurgitating something people could find through a simple Google search. It doesn't really matter if you want to inspire, educate, or entertain, make sure you do it in story form.

Tip #2: Summarize your research and make the information applicable to your target market. Make sure they have a takeaway they can actually implement. If you're writing something inspirational, make sure it has an action attached. We can't just tell people, "You're great, you're enough, hope you feel good." You have to give them actionable steps or else they'll forget what you said in mere minutes.

Tip #3: Be detailed. If you're giving step-by-step instructions, this is especially important or people will flood you with 5,000 of the same exact question and then you'll be forced to start drinking wine at an inappropriate time of day and your family will judge you. Just be detailed.

Tip #4: Don't use twenty words where two will do. Don't waste people's time. Get in and get out. Have a point to every sentence and don't worry so much about how people will interpret your writing. Someone will hate everything you write, so just embrace it. Did you know that Facebook posts with less than 81 words gets 66% more engagement? Keep it simple.

Tip #5: Embrace your YOU-ness. Write like you talk. Make your posts conversational so your audience can hear your voice as they read your words. They'll stay around longer if it doesn't feel like a computer talking. They'll also trust you a little more if you talk about your product in your own words rather than some cheesy sales voice you think you're supposed to use.

Tip #6: Make your regulars your priority. I read the comments about 99% of the time after I write something. I try to respond if I can. I have a friend, Carrie Colbert, who is excellent at responding to her Instagram comments on her Wear Where Well feed. She does a great job making the people who take the time to comment feel special. Try to take note of everyone who is interacting with you so you can make those people a priority when it comes to your time.

Tip #7: I want people to know I see them when they interact on my posts. On Facebook and Instagram, I "like" each post after I read them so they know I saw their words and effort to connect.

Tip #8: There are some internet experts who will tell you to do a 70/30 split on your promotions on social media. Meaning 70% of your content is engaging readers and 30% is promotion of your product. I think that's way high. I don't stick around for the 70% if 30% is about sales. I personally stick to 80/20 at a minimum, and I'd suggest aiming for 90/10. I really do think your content needs to be more engaging than it needs to be about sales.

Tip #9: Make it prettier. A picture every. single. time. No exception.

## Schedule

The point of scheduling social media posts is to keep you moving forward. It is about having something written in advance and posting on the day you've scheduled it for. The reason I would even ask you to do something like this is for one reason and one reason only — consistency. If you want regular followers, you're going to need to be posting on the regular. When you go radio silent for weeks at a time and then come back to ten posts a day, people get whiplash and they'll miss so much. Give people a little bit of your brand every single day so your product is fresh on their mind when they finally decide today is the day they need it.

Let me give you an example of a time this worked for another company where I was the consumer. Hello Apparel (www.hellomerch.com). Who doesn't love their stuff? I think it's adorable, but I'm hesitant to buy tee shirts online because I only like the softest kinds of tee shirts. (I'm like the worst kind of tee shirt snob. If it itches, I'll throw it away. If I order an XL and you send me something that would fit on my infant daughter, I'll curse you and then throw it away. Clearly, I've been burned a time or two in the tee shirt department.) Hello is really good at their social media timing and consistency. One morning they posted the rainbow tee shirt I had been looking at for months and it was just the right time for me to buy that particular morning. I had to see it multiple times in my feed to finally decide to click "buy." Make sure you're consistent when you post because you never know when it's going to be the day to click the buy button for someone who has seen your product many times before. PS. The Hello tees are amazingly soft and comfy. Lindsay approved.

There are many really convenient ways to schedule your posts. One is through an ancient and forgotten practice called writing it on a calendar. It's a dinosaur, but it works. The great thing about your digital calendar is that it will (in theory) sync to all of your devices so you'll have access to the schedule at any time. Apparently having a planner is cool again so you could always use one of those as well if the calendar is too small or you're into hand-writing your ideas out. Plus, when you use a planner there's a good chance you'll get to also use washi tape and that's a win. Finally, there are some apps that will help you not only schedule what you'll be writing about, but they'll actually go and physically push your content onto your desired platform of choice at the time you wish it to be posted. It's like magic! A little word of warning, I find there are some people in my line of work that are super passionate about intentionally ignoring posts that are put onto Facebook through an automated system. I can't say I understand it, but to each his own. Here are some apps for you to look into if you need help scheduling and posting your content. I'm not going to give you a lot of in-depth pricing information about them because by the time you read this, there's a good chance they've gotten an update. Do some research on the different options to find out which one is right for your business and budget at this time.

**Hootsuite** — www.hootsuite.com

**Buffer** — www.buffer.com

**Sprout Social** — www.sproutsocial.com

**Viral Heat** — www.viralheat.com

**SocialOomph** — www.socialoomph.com

**TweetDeck** — www.tweetdeck.com

**Sprinklr** — www.sprinklr.com

**Social Pilot** — www.socialpilot.co

**Send Social Media** — www.sendsocialmedia.com

**SalesForce Marketing Cloud** — www.marketingcloud.com

# PLATFORMS | 4

# PART FOUR:

# Platforms

There are so many social media platforms now that I could literally use up all of the words allotted to me for this book just talking to you about them. I'm not going to do that because, Google. What I am going to do is focus on the major contenders. The platforms that are here today will likely be here tomorrow, too. That doesn't mean my list is where you must be. You can choose the right platform

**YOU CAN CHOOSE**

**THE RIGHT PLATFORM FOR YOU**

**by narrowing down**

*where your audience*

**SPENDS MOST OF THEIR TIME ONLINE**

for you by narrowing down where your audience spends most of their time online. I spend most of my time on Instagram and Facebook because my audience is visual and craves personal connection. There are a lot of great platforms that are up and coming and you may choose to spend your time trying to reach customers there. For the sake of simplicity, I'm going to be focusing on five major places to reach new customers:

1. Blogs

2. Facebook

3. Instagram

4. Twitter

5. Pinterest

I realize I'm leaving out LinkedIn. That's because I hate LinkedIn. I don't get it. There, I said it. Probably not the best thing to read from someone who you're depending on to teach you, I just haven't found it to be usable and relevant in my business yet. Also, I wouldn't talk about something I absolutely have no idea about. I'm also leaving out SnapChat, which I do like, but I am having a hard time connecting the platform to actual sales because of the limited data I get on my followers and general user unfriendliness. Plus, InstaStory - bye SnapChat. I think of SnapChat as a great way to grow the brand of you and be able to let people into little snippets of your life. With the addition of Instagram Stories though? Well…I kinda kicked SnapChat out of bed for reasons of simplicity and consolidation only.

## Blogs

The first thing I want to say is that it's not a requirement to have a blog to create a successful business. In the past five years I've cut way down on the amount of blogs I read regularly to almost none…actually, that's a lie. It's none. I don't read a single blog regularly. I've replaced it solely with Instagram and Facebook. However, a blog is still a great way to interact with your customers and give them more information than a small post and a photo on social media. The thing about the blog is that I believe it needs to constantly be referenced on another platform now.

Back when I first dabbled in social media, in the ancient year of 2005, people would start their day by running through their blog roll and reading what was new. I believe that's an activity of the past. Now we read blogs when the writer has given us a little snippet of the content and then posts a link for us to get more information. Studying the interaction on my own blog, I can see the activity spike when I include a link to the blog post with a compelling reason for my audience to click the link. The blog market is saturated. Everyone and everything has a blog associated with it. In 2005, that might have been a different story. We need to make sure we adapt to changing markets and we're being smart about where we're putting our time and efforts.

The biggest piece of advice I have for any businessperson that who is thinking about starting or continuing a blog is to not let your product take it over if you're just a one-man-show. Once you get bigger and you get some employees under your belt, sure, your product line might be diverse enough to create content consistently throughout the year about

## A BLOG IS A GREAT WAY

### FOR YOU TO LET YOUR CUSTOMERS

and your potential customers

### IN ON WHO YOU ARE

*and what you love*

it. In the beginning though? I think a blog is a great way for you to let your customers and potential customers in on who you are and what you love. If your product and your business is one of those things, great. If it's the only thing, well, then it starts to feel like a sales tactic. When I feel like a blog is constantly trying to ram a product

down my throat and I'm not learning anything from the posts, I'm out.

Here are my blog tips for people who are really hustling to get their product or service sold:

1. Make a list of the things you're good at and you could teach someone about. Blog about those things. For example, I love photography, scrapbooking, being a momtrepreneur, and my family. I can teach people about the first 3 things because I'm pretty dang good at them. The last one? I'm a work in progress, but I'm willing to be honest about my shortcomings in the parenting and wife-ing departments. I think people are attracted to the honesty. What I don't do is constantly blog about the product I sell. It's part of what I blog about every so often, but it's not a main theme. I want people to come for the content about our common

interests and stay through the parts where I discuss my product or service. As I mentioned earlier, it's easier, once people get to know me a little bit, to make the leap between our common interests and their likely interest in what I sell as well.

2. Speaking of honesty, I challenge you to be brutally honest if you're going to write a blog. I don't think I'm alone in saying that if I have to read another blog about a mom who has 2.5 perfect children with perfect hair who fart rainbows and ride unicorns in their free time, I'm going to throw my MacBook out the window (JK, I'd throw my wallet out the window first). For the love of God, people, let's just tell our stories flaws and all. I promise you the ugly, vulnerable, imperfect, messy posts I make get way more attention than the ones where I look like the hero. People want to know they're not alone. By telling the real story, they'll know they can trust you because you were honest with the crap that nobody's talking about. I'm sorry, but no, you did not wake up like that. You got ready for 3.5 hours before you took that picture of yourself in the bathroom mirror, friend. Your lack of mascara residue and the fact that you have pants on are giving you away. Be real yo! People appreciate it.

3. Be consistent. Just as you'll need to be consistent and have a wide variety of content for your social media feeds, the same rings true for your blog. Once a week isn't enough. Organize, plan, write and schedule.

4. Write in your authentic tone of voice. I try my hardest to write exactly as I would talk, even if it's not grammatically correct all the time.

As long as my audience can understand it and they can hear me in the words, I'm on the right track. I think this is another little trick that builds trust, especially if people have heard me speak. It connects them to me and they can start to get to know the real me.

5. Don't rip people off. I shouldn't really have to write this because, you know, we're all adults. But I think for new bloggers there are a lot of rules about what's legal and what's not and it can be confusing. So I'll spell out a few things I see fairly often here for all of us as a refresher. First, make sure your words are your own. If you like a quote from another blog or book or anywhere else, make sure you're crediting the original writer. Second, just because it's on Google images doesn't mean you can use it. I actually didn't know this when I first started blogging. You can purchase stock images but you cannot use images that are other people's from the internet. It's basically stealing and they can actually sue you for their intellectual property rights. Just stay away from it. Create your own images or buy the rights to an image if you're going to be posting images. Finally, if you saw the idea somewhere else and you'd like to basically copy it, ask them and give credit. I know I get really frustrated when I see someone basically take my idea and slap his or her name on it (it will happen to all of us at one time or another). It's just frustrating. Let's avoid that and respect those that came before us.

## Facebook

Post frequency: 1-3 times a day

Optimal days: Weekdays + Sunday

Optimal time: 1:00-4:00pm Central or Eastern Time

When it comes to Facebook, make sure you're packing a punch with your posts. Too long and too many frustrates readers. Keep them short and make sure you're including a good mix of personal, business, and education. There are three different ways to use Facebook for your business.

1. Facebook Profile

2. Facebook Page

3. Facebook Group

## Facebook Profile

I use my Facebook profile to post regular updates. If you're a regular Instagram user, you can actually connect the two so that when you post an Instagram photo, it can be shared over to your Facebook profile. Genius. For your regular Facebook posts that go onto your wall, make sure you keep it short and sweet. In general, unless what you're saying is really entertaining, people won't make it through the whole post if it's long. In fact, people actually only make it through 24% of your Facebook statuses so make them really short and draw people in quick.

## Facebook Page

I think Facebook pages are one of the most misused business tools. I'm in the camp that your business brand and your personal brand should intermingle. For most small-business owners, if your main Facebook page is public, that will serve just fine. Facebook is actually going to want you to pay to put your posts in front of people once you get that official page, so it doesn't make sense from an analytics standpoint right away. You'll know a page is right for you if your friend quota starts filling up (5,000 friends is the limit) and you're having a hard time keeping up with the people you know and love on your profile. The only way I see it working for you as a one-man-show is if you are willing to connect your personal social media feeds to that one and you're committed to making sure you're posting there frequently. For people like me, that means having to post in two different locations most times; once on my profile for my friends to see and another on my page so that my customers and potential customers can see.

My caveat to the Facebook page is for people in direct sales. It is my personal opinion that if you're trying to sell a product that is not yours, a Facebook page will not really help you. You're going to want to be connecting to your warm market and that's people that actually know you. A Facebook page in the direct sales world attracts other members to it to check out what you're doing. Those people are your competition and you're not creating content for them. You're creating content for your potential and current customers. Really look into who might follow your Facebook page before you set one up and analyze if it's the right choice for your business.

## Facebook Group

This may be the most common way I use Facebook. I love my groups. This is a place where I can get all of my customers and potential customers together in a private space and let them talk to each other about the product. I can teach people things here and don't have to worry about putting too much unusable content in the feeds of the people who don't need to see it. You can adjust the settings for your group to make them public, private or secret. There are a lot of features that groups are missing and I believe you'll still need a blog for certain things but groups can be a great way to connect with your people in a more intimate space.

## Instagram

Post frequency: 1-3 times a day

Optimal days: Every day of the week

Optimal time: 11:00am-2:00pm Central or Eastern Time

Instagram is my social media platform of choice. I get better traction on my Instagram posts than I do my Facebook posts at this time. Last year I set out to increase my following on purpose and saw an amazing jump just by doing a few simple things consistently. The thing I love most about Instagram is that it forces us to use a picture every single time.

Since it's something we should be doing anyway, I love it. I believe if you're not on Instagram right now, you're handicapping your business. Don't resist it. Go set up an account if you haven't already.

Make sure you include a good mix of all topics in your Instagram posts. Hashtags work really well to bring in quality followers. Make sure you add two hashtags in the main description of your image and then put any additional ones you'd like to include in the comments section to cut down on the amount people feel they have to read.

**ONE THING I DO O**

# INSTAGRA

more than any other platform

*to interact with peopl*

THAT COMMENT ON MY IMAGI

Just as you would be real on your blog, make sure you're being authentic on your Instagram account. There's such a pull to paint a completely perfect picture of our lives and our business on Instagram because so many other people do it. Don't compare your story to other people's. Be who you are and watch the people come to check out your feed regularly. One thing I do on Instagram more than any other platform is interact with people that comment on my images. I want them to know I've seen their post. It's worth the time to do it. Finally, make sure you take the time to place quality images on your Instagram feed because that will determine if people read your description or interact with you. It's all done on a snap judgment based on the picture you choose, so choose wisely. We'll talk more later on about how to create great images but know that more than any other platform your Instagram images need to be on point.

## Twitter

Post frequency: 5-7 times a day

Optimal days: Every day of the week

Optimal time: 1:00-3:00pm Central or Eastern Time

The great thing about Twitter is that the content is so short so you can post more frequently. Make sure you save your most important content for the optimal times. I have a hard time following Twitter because it moves so fast, but that's also the beauty of it. You can post short snippets with a link to get people moved to a platform where you have more room to give more information; direct them to your blog posts, direct them to your Instagram images. Almost everyone is or has been on Twitter at this point and it certainly is a good way to pepper your customers with more short bursts of information to keep you on their mind. I think the 140-character limit also makes us become more creative about how we're saying what we need to say. I like the way that confinement feels sometimes when I start to tire of writing too much.

## Pinterest

Pin frequency: 10-25 times a day

Optimal days: Every day of the week

Optimal time: Weekday evenings and Weekend mornings

Pinterest is the place I go when I need blog recommendations for a project or idea. The great thing about it is that you can mix in your own content with other things you like so people get to know that your feed is a good place for recommendations. You can pin and re-pin a lot of things on Pinterest because, like Twitter, the feed moves fast. People won't read long descriptions so save the extra information for the linked content. Make sure you're pinning the post every time you blog and that you're covering a wide range of topics on your pin boards so you're pulling in a wider audience. Pin information about or concerning your product or market to make sure you're pulling in your target customers.

# 5
—
# THE SOCIAL MEDIA MUST-HAVES

# PART FIVE:

# The Social Media Must-Haves

Alright, now for the fun part. This is where you combine your unique personality and skills into something that people want to read and are pulled to engage with. In this section we're going to talk about all of the ways you can turn up the volume on your posts and get them in front of more people. Before we get into the specifics I want you to know a couple of things.

## Know Your Worth

Most importantly you should know that your worth is not determined by the number of likes or followers or comments or compliments you get in a day. Those things feel good for approximately 1.2 seconds and then they're gone. Likewise, your worth is not determined by the number of people who hate everything you do. Those things, I find, stick around for a lot longer if you let them. Just remember, rude internet people don't know you and don't care about you. Your product is not you, it's just something you love and want to share with the world.

Let me be totally honest with you: I have poured years of my life completely into my business trying to make sure what I do helps other people. I can say my business decisions and actions come from a sincere and genuine place. Still, there are people that line up to join the I Hate Lindsay Club. It might even be a popular club. Believe it or not, some of the stuff they might say about me may be completely false, but some of it would be, (gasp), true! I am a flawed, broken, imperfect person. Most of those people, though? They don't know me at all. They don't see the hours I put in and the motive behind my actions. Many people on the internet forget that a person with feelings is sitting on the other side of every comment they make. Know that when you do something brave and you put your heart out for people to judge, you're going to get hurt. My honest feelings about this are to let this teach you a lesson when you're tempted to criticize on the internet. One of my favorite quotes by Rachel Wolchin is, "Maturing is realizing how many things don't require your comment."

just remember

# RUDE

INTERNET PEOPLE

*don't know you*

and don't care

ABOUT YOU

Just let it go, friends. Michael has to remind me more than I want to admit when I want to spit back at some jerk behind a computer.

When I receive criticism or negative and hurtful comments, I try to keep these things in mind. First, their actions or words are about them and not me. Their words are about their past hurts and feelings. The anger may be directed at me, but it's not about me. It's a symptom of a bigger issue and I don't know that issue and I can't judge that issue. I come from a rough, broken home. There are things I do and ways I behave in certain situations that are broken because of it. I'm sure I hurt people all the time while I build walls to protect myself. That's about me and not them. As I've been on the receiving end of some real verbal ass-beatings in the past couple of years, I've become more sensitive to how I hurt people and I now appreciate the people who love me even more. It's been a learning experience that I had to walk through to understand.

I'm not saying that harsh words get easier to hear (no, they do not). I'm saying that it becomes easier to understand. Brené Brown said in her book, Rising Strong, "What if we believed that everyone was doing the best they could?" Can I tell you honestly that I stopped reading that book after that part because it opened such a deep wound in my little girl heart? I had a father who purposefully hurt me and a mother who watched it happen. How can I say they were both doing the best they could if my sole dependence was on them for protection? That question burned me up and it made me cry, but there was also truth in it. Maybe my mom and dad, however imperfect and flawed, were just doing the best they were capable of. I challenge you, when someone says something that makes you want to go off and drink hard whiskey to forget…like in a country bar or something…to ask yourself, "What if they're just doing the best they can?" What if they're just not equipped yet to handle the strong feelings they obviously have about your product and therefore you? Could you give yourself the grace to ask yourself the same question? "I was just doing the best I could with the information and experience I had." Mistakes happen. People get hurt. We're just doing the best we can.

## Build Your Skill

Look, building a social media presence isn't something you snap your fingers and get. You're not going to finish this book and magically have 1,000 good followers when you're done. The hardest part about finding that perfect spot where what you say is noticed by a lot of people is going to take some trial and error. You're going to have to make a lot of mistakes (publicly) to know what works for you and what doesn't. It's not always fun but guys, it's the way; social media is the way. There's never

there's never been an *easier and cheaper way* TO GENUINELY CONNECT WITH **AN AUDIENCE** THAN THROUGHOUT THE INVENTION OF **SOCIAL MEDIA** been an easier and cheaper way to genuinely connect with an audience than through the invention of social media. There are skills you'll need to learn in order to be successful and hit that sweet spot where the words flow and the photos pop. You'll have to practice a lot. The reward is there if you will do the work. Take the classes, accept the feedback (not all hard feedback is internet hate…sometimes it's actually love in the form of hard things we don't want to hear), try new things, abandon plans, go out on a limb, be vulnerable, observe people who are doing it right. You got this. Building a successful social media presence is part of the long marathon that you're running to get your product to the people. Hear me, we need your product. We need you to do this. Just keep trying.

Alright, now that we have that out of the way, let's talk about the must-have characteristics of a good social media feed. Squeeeeeee, I'm so excited! I'm not just writing that, I really am excited. My heart started beating faster just at the thought of writing this stuff. Embrace the nerdery.

## Relatability

Okay, lesson one: your posts need to be relatable to your audience. They have to be able to see themselves in what you post, what you say, how you say it and how you present your information. Think about a comedian. Some of the funniest things they present are hilarious because they're true. We can see our actions and ourselves in the joke. We can laugh because we relate. The same is going to have to be true for your feed. I don't follow the girl that has it all together because that just makes me feel bad about the shit show that is my life on most days. I don't follow the mom whose kids brush their teeth without being screamed at because, let's be honest, I basically have to wrestle the thing into my kids' mouths every night. I don't follow the business owner who always wins. That's just not my reality. Those things make me start to compare their life to mine and I lose that battle every time. Also, they're liars. I don't want to buy things from liars.

There's this fine line that you're going to have to find in your daily posts where you present yourself as the expert, because y'are, but you also aren't afraid to show the times in your life where things just don't work out. Your audience needs to remember that you're also human. I believe we follow people on social media because they have a certain something we're looking for. Either they inspire us, they teach us something, they entertain us, or they live a life that we want a little piece of for our own. The great thing about it is that if you're just true to your story, the real story, people are going to inherently want a piece of your good life. They'll want to do the things you do, and have the things you have, because it will give them what they perceive as the good life. I actually love this part of social media as long as it doesn't become a comparison game. I love getting recommendations from people I know have amazing interior decorating style. I love getting parenting advice from women who are wiser than I am. I love watching the feed and feeling inspired by Christian women who know my spiritual struggles. So don't be afraid to tell the good and the bad. Don't believe the lie that if it's not all a perfect picture tied with a perfect satin bow, it's not useful to your audience. Be relatable.

## What's the Story?

Lesson two: tell us a story. Imagine yourself as a little five-year-old in pigtails crawling up on your daddy's lap for another story. The same story you've heard thousands of times. Again. Again! Maybe this is part of your nightly routine. It is in my house. Mine, however, are smarter than me and they'll pull the story card when it's lights out time knowing mom guilt is the strongest weapon in their bag of tricks. GO TO SLEEP, TINY SATAN! That escalated quickly. Look, just because you're not five anymore doesn't mean you don't have that same desire to be told a story, to get lost in another reality. You're going to have to learn the art of telling a story to your followers.

They want it.

They crave it.

We go to movies, we read books, we get lost in fictional worlds; we want a good story. Some of us use it as motivation, inspiration, and escapism. Don't just state the facts, present them in a story form. Help them get into what it feels like to be you today and then show them how your product can help them in their life like it did you. Your product or service likely meets a need. Present that need in story form. Help them connect to you on an emotional level and buying will become so much easier.

There are a couple of kinds of stories you can tell on your feed. I think most of them should just be about your life and who you are rather than about what you do and what you sell. Tell your story. Tell your family's story. Tell your customer's story. Tell the awesome and tell the tough. You can also tell stories about your product. The way I do that is to present a story about my life and I sprinkle the product in. My product isn't the main event, it's just something that makes doing life easier. It's going to make reading about your product a whole lot more entertaining than reading some facts and figures. Remember, people are really buying who you are and why your product exists rather than what you do and what your product does.

There's more to telling a story than just writing out the words that describe an event. There are some pieces of a story that need to be present in order to get people to read it. One of the pieces of that story is the lead character. Donald Miller refers to it as the hero in his Story Brand talks. If you haven't read or watched Donald Miller, I expect that to be your next move after finishing this book. Mmmmkay, moving on.

Did you know that every good (and satisfying) story has a main character or hero, a goal, a conflict, a guide and a moral? Think about all of the

**IF YOU HAVEN'T** *read or watched* **DONALD MILLER** i expect that to be YOUR NEXT MOVE AFTER FINISHING THIS BOOK

epic summer blockbusters. These parts of that story are generally not hard to recognize. Any movie that you walk out of feeling satisfied has these parts. Think about Star Wars. Think about Harry Potter. Think about The Hunger Games. Think actual superhero movies. Every romantic comedy ever produced. It's all there. In our stories, it's super easy to make ourselves the hero. I find this especially true when it comes to this business. We want to show others how amazing this business is and how much our product and business has connected us to our dreams. So we tell our story. Logically, when we tell our story, we tell them our struggles and how we overcame and we tell them how much better we feel at the end. The problem with that is that we're missing the chance to make our customer or friend the hero in the story.

If you want to sell something, you need to make sure you're making your customer or friend the hero in the story. As people who have gone first, we need to be putting ourselves into the mentorship role. When I learned that, I wanted to punch myself in the face because it's so simple and so profound. Our people need to see themselves in our story and we need to take their hand so that they can be the hero in their story. Not us. When we tell stories, we need to be reaching our hand out to take on the mentor role in the story of the people we know and love. We need to make their story shine. What does that look like?

It looks like telling the story of other people, not just ourselves.

It looks like putting ourselves in their situation and understanding them.

It looks like telling them we're here to help.

It looks like telling them we're here to link arms with them instead of trying to manipulate them into a sale.

It looks like showing them that it's not about one sale; it's about making sure your product works in their life.

It looks like reading your words from the customer's perspective.

it's not about **THE PRODUCT** it's about being *inspired*

As you tell your story on social media, I want you to position your reader as the hero. I want you to continue to do that over and over and over. With this simple switch, you can capture attention, entertain, enlighten, and persuade all in the course of just a few minutes. Remember it's not about you! It's about them.

## Inspire Your Followers

Lesson three: inspire people. I believe people want to be inspired into saying yes to something. What is it that inspired you to create your business? What is it going to do in your life? What do you know it can do for others? What have you learned that you can use to inspire others in their lives because, peeps, life is really, really hard sometimes? When I first started my business, I did it because I felt hopelessly alone as a mom of three little girls that couldn't hold a conversation with me yet. I was bored, I was tired, I wasn't fulfilled, I was often angry, and I was ashamed to admit it because good moms don't talk like that about the mom life.

I was inspired to admit that I kinda hated my life and I didn't feel like I contributed to my family in a way that used my gifts and talents. I was inspired to create a place where other moms could come alongside me to have a place not only to talk to other adults and use their talents, but also to link arms with other people who believe what they believe. I was inspired to create a space to build my own business and help other women do the same. You know what happens when I tell that story? It inspires others to do more of the same. That inspiration has spread and created a multi-million dollar producing business. It's not about the product; it's about being inspired. The product works and I love it so much I have it stashed in every single room in my house. But my business wasn't built on product alone. It was built on common connection to other women. As you teach people the lessons you've learned, remember to inspire them to be more, to be better, to be the best versions of themselves. Come alongside them and help them with shortcuts to life – the life of their dreams – as you've had others teach you. I'll do pretty much anything to inspire my people because I know it leads to their personal fulfillment and success for everyone. Just try to stop a woman who has a fire burning way down deep inside her soul. It's magic.

## Sell the Right Thing

Lesson four: sell the hole and not the drill. I beat this concept into the heads of the people who follow me. When I give business advice, this one is always a part of it. In fact, my "people" are probably rolling their eyes at hearing it again. Get used to it, friends, it's sticking around. When you buy a drill, are you really buying a piece of hardware made of plastic and steel that plugs into your wall? No, you're buying a hole. Just a hole. People don't buy drills, they buy holes. All that money for a hole. When you look at commercials for power tools, what do they show you? The sleek design of that power tool? Maybe a little, but more often it's a completed home project. It's the picture of the husband and wife with a cup of coffee and a dog standing together admiring their perfectly put together home. They're selling the home. They're selling how you'll feel once you use that drill. You'll see that vision of the happy homeowners and your mind skips right over the fact that you'll probably drill 16 holes in your wall to get it right (and cover it with a large picture, amiright?)

and you'll think you need that exact drill to make your home renovating dreams come true.

Too often we get caught up in all the pieces of our product or service, and we don't spend enough time painting a picture of what people are really buying and the effect it will have on their life or the lives of the people they love. As you have conversations with your potential customers or followers, ask more questions, do less talking. Get to know your customers on an emotional level, and you'll be able to make sure you continue meeting their needs. Identify their underlying need and talk about it. You might get a lot of attention on social media if you just come right out and talk about what you see your customers are dealing with and how the product might help. Here are a few questions you might start off asking yourself about potential customers as they're trying to decide whether your product is a good investment for them at this time. If you don't have the answers, perhaps asking them is the right next step.

What will your product do for them?

How will it affect their lives?

Why do they need this now?

How might their needs change once they have the product?

What is their emotional connection to this product or service?

It doesn't matter how surface level you think your product is, there's an emotional connection to it. It's going to meet some kind of need, even if it's a personal one. I have an emotional connection to the dishwasher

I bought this year. I wanted to make sure I'd be able to get help if there was ever an issue. I wanted to make sure it wasn't going to ruin my brand new hardwood floors after a year. I wanted to know that my pain point mattered to the company I was buying from. People want to know they matter. They want to be heard. If you give them an opportunity to be heard and to know they matter, not only will they continue to buy your product, but they'll convince others to buy it, too. Spend more time with your customers when they email you or comment on your posts. Paint them the picture of what their life could be like with your product.

## Understand Your Customer's Pain Points

Lesson five: understand the underlying need and offer solutions. You wanna be great at sales? You can be. It's a skill. Like many skills, some are taught early without asking (which is how I learned a lot about sales... through watching) and some you have to learn on purpose. Selling is a skill. One big part of this skill is being able to identify the customer's pain point. Yesterday I was watching a little web video intro to a workshop I'm getting ready to do, and the instructor brought up pain points. I wanted to stand and clap for him. "All the yes!" I wanted to shout, "You get it!" We sometimes refer to a pain point as an underlying need and I've touched on it in the previous section about selling the hole instead of the drill. It's basically a part of a person's life that causes them pain, be it physical or not. Knowing what causes our customer's pain is integral to our businesses if we want to sustain them. We need to get to know our customer.

Here's a little excerpt from an INC Magazine article I love: "Pain is a reminder that unless your prospect has a need to solve a problem, they are not going to buy a product. Customers sometimes buy things spontaneously without thinking through what they actually need. But, often, there is an underlying reason for a purchase, even if the buyer doesn't bring it to the surface."

So, the next question you should ask is, how do you know your customer's pain point?

I'm going to answer that question by telling you what not to do. This is something I see all the time on social media. It's really profound; I hope you're ready for it.

Stop making it all about you.

Telling your story is awesome and something you should be doing. Your stories should be told as a way to connect, not a way to simply talk about yourself. When it comes to telling a story about your product, just saying, "I love this product/service" isn't attracting people. You're just saying something to hear yourself talk at that point and the more you do that, the more people scroll right past your posts without so much as reading a word. Your posts have to have a point, and the object of every post should be to connect through a common pain point. Your pain is their pain and if that's true, you get them. If you're selling something, what you say cannot be about you, it needs to be about them. How many social media feeds do you come across that become all about the person writing? I can make you a list right now. Where's the WIIFM (what's in it for me)? Mark Sussta calls this action "crocodile-ing;" really big mouth and really small ears. Listen to your customers, they'll tell you their pain. Make it your mission to put yourself in their shoes.

Identifying your customer's pain points is actually only half of the equation, though. The second half is offering them a solution. It wasn't enough for me to know that moms feel lonely during the day and trapped without the ability to say how they really feel about staying at home with toddlers all day. I had to bring that pain into the light and give them a solution. If only there was a place where fellow moms could come together in a common purpose to meet new people and help contribute to the household all while still staying at home with their kids. Oh, hold up. There is. It's my job to talk about it, and so I did. And you know what happened? People jumped on board. They said yes. They gave my product and service a try. I offer the solution to my people through my story. Not in a hard sell, but in a true, authentic story, and I paint the picture for them about what it could look like for other women who might feel the same.

## Create Action

Lesson six: now that you know the components of getting attention for your posts, you need to tell your customer what to do. That sounds pretty #LadyBoss, but in my experience, people just want to be told what to do. They want it to be simple and they want to have it spoon-fed to them. I'm not saying be harsh. I'm saying, tell them what the next steps are and show them how to find it. If you want people to go read a blog post, give them the link. If you want them to purchase your product, show them how. Ask for the sale. You've done a good job showing them the value it can bring to their life, it's okay to tell them what the next step is without them thinking you're a self-serving jerk who's just trying to make a buck.

I think Jon Acuff does a great job of this on his blog. Somewhere in most of his posts you'll find a link to his New York Times Bestseller. He's not afraid to tell you to go buy it because what he just served you was helpful. If you liked what he just wrote, there's also a good chance you'll also like his book. It makes sense. He's a businessman and it's his job to sell his book. You're a businessperson; it's your job to sell your product or service. Don't be afraid to do it. Sales is only creepy if it's done wrong. Since your posts are relatable, written in story form, inspirational, and focused on helping the customer, you've set yourself up to be able to ask for the sale in a totally non-used-car-salesman way.

# 6

# BRING IT DOWN A NOTCH

# PART SIX:

# Bring It Down a Notch

"Many brands lead consumers down confusing purchase paths. The savviest ones simplify and personalize the route." -Harvard Business Review

One of the things I kept finding myself wanting to tell people over and over and over again is to simplify everything. The past six months or so I've had to take my own advice as far as simplifying goes and I've noticed how over-complicated everything surrounding my product and business can become. It's like I believe I have to make it more complicated so that people will think it's legit. In truth, I actually believe the opposite. I believe the simpler you can make it, the easier it is for others to see how it may fit into their lives. Sure, there are some complexities to your product or service, but those things can also be made simple if communicated in the right way. Then the customer gets the chance to dive deeper and get more information if it's what they want.

When I first started my business I knew that my target market wasn't going to have time to do a lot of research on my product and they weren't going to get into something with a steep learning curve, so I set out to make everything really easy for them. Teach them just what they need to know to get started and then let them decide how much more information they need. I credit that move as a major reason we were able to grow from 1 to 300,000 customers in just a couple of years. Simplicity sells.

Here's a little piece of a Harvard Business Review article I read a while back about a survey they did: "Our study bored in on what makes consumers 'sticky'—that is, likely to follow through on an intended purchase, buy the product repeatedly, and recommend it to others. We looked at the impact on stickiness of more than 40 variables, including price, customers' perceptions of a brand, and how often consumers interacted with the brand. The single biggest driver of stickiness, by far, was 'decision simplicity'—the ease with which consumers can gather trustworthy information about a product and confidently and efficiently weigh their purchase options. What consumers want from marketers is, simply, simplicity."

Simplicity makes customers sticky -- meaning, they're most likely to click the "buy" button and then not only repeat buy, but also recommend our product/service.

We must simplify every part of our process from how we describe our product to how it's purchased.

Is there a way to streamline your email marketing?

What can you do to track your customers so you can send them more personalized content?

Is there a follow-up email you can send to each customer to help simplify common questions?

Is there a way you can take some of the mystery out of the product up front to help convince them the product is for them?

Can you add something to the packaging to help clear up confusion?

Can you take out a bunch of words on your website to consolidate information and make it easy for them?

Is your sign-up/buy process overly complicated?

Can you give people simpler information all the way through your process?

Do whatever you have to do to make the process of trying, buying, re-buying, and sharing your product easier. If you can master simplicity, you'll not only like your job more because it will be more organized, but your customers will be able to respond to your product offerings more often.

# IMAGE IS EVERYTHING

# 7

## PART 7:

# Image is Everything

One hard and fast rule I have for social media (outside of Twitter, of course) is that a picture, image or video is required.

Always.

One study on Facebook interaction found that photos get 104% more comments and 53% more likes than posts with no photo. They're important. The more visually stunning you can make your posts, the more people will be attracted to it and want to know about it. While it's more convenient than ever to take photos with our phones and devices, it also opens the door to some images that don't tell the whole story about your product because, let's be honest, the average phone photo just sucks. There are tons of ways you can make your phone pictures work for your business, but most people don't understand their device fully and they don't know how to take a well-crafted image. It's time to learn. I'm going to give you some tips on taking better photos with that phone so you're more prepared to wow your readers with your images. If you really want to step up your game, you can learn how to use an SLR camera. You should know you'll probably either learn it yourself or you should be prepared to hire someone to help you with the images of your product in the future. If you really want to take your skill to the next level, there are some amazing classes for you to check out online. I've seen some amazing results from online workshops for both photography and videography, which we'll be talking about in this section. Checkout the workshop lineup from the following websites:

**SkillShare** — www.skillshare.com

**Creative Live** — www.creativelive.com

**ClickinMoms** — www.clickinmoms.com/cmu

## Photos

An iPhone will never take the place of an SLR camera, but I realize not everybody knows how to use one or has the desire to ever pick up such a complicated gadget. I get it. You can still get some great images from your iPhone, especially with the updates Apple makes to their cameras every year. I can't speak to the Android devices because I'm pretty sure my heart is actually shaped like the Apple logo. Apple and me were meant to be. Here are a few tips on taking photos of both your everyday world and your product to help you get noticed a bit more on social media.

1. Clean up the background. My mom was a real estate agent. She would always tell her clients when she went to help them list their house that they needed to remove everything from their horizontal surfaces but the absolute necessities. Clean canvases sell. The same rings true for photography. Before you take pictures of your product, take notice of what's in the background of your view finder simply by paying attention to it. Remove all toys from inside of the frame. Make sure you get rid of that two-day-old Diet Coke that you haven't gotten into the trash yet. I'm not saying your house needs to be perfect or that you need to fake a perfectly neat home, but if you're trying to showcase a product, make it the star by removing the clutter.

2. Find interesting backdrops. The easiest one on the planet is to run down to Walgreens and grab some white posterboard. Boom instant clean background and shooting from above is so right now. Add a couple of little props in to accent your product and you're ready to roll. Simply move your camera in or out by physically moving your body (please don't use the zoom on your camera, that just wrecks the quality) or cropping the photo in post-production. In the biz, they call that "post" and we're cool so we're going to call it post, too. Another great idea is to run down to the hardware store and grab some pieces of stone and wood to fake a different surface in the home. Just because you don't have a house full of

perfect wood floors doesn't mean you can't shoot your product on some wood. You can even purchase paper backgrounds that look like wood if you find yourself using them a lot and want something a little lighter to lug around.

3. Move your product close to a window for more natural light. That light that pours through your window is gold, take advantage of it. Shooting into the light can even be really interesting and add some nice sun flair to your photo. Make sure you put your finger on the subject of the photo so your camera knows where the light should be. If you shoot into a window without telling your camera where the subject is, you'll notice that often your subject can come out almost black. Simply locking the focus on your subject will help you light up the right part of the photo.

4. Know the rule of thirds. This is a design "rule" where you break up your viewfinder into a grid with 9 boxes on it. Your phone has a handy tool you can use to see your grid as you're taking photos. To turn it on, simply go to Settings>Photos & Camera and then turn on the slider next to Grid. You should now notice it when you click the camera on your phone like you're going to take a picture. You'll probably also notice it when you take pictures in the square format. This is a tool to help you balance your photo so it's the most appealing to the viewer. The rule of thumb is to put important parts of the picture along those lines. When I take a picture of a person, I try to put their eyes on that top horizontal

line and then position their body either on one of the two vertical lines or directly in the center. You should try the same with a product. Position whatever is the most important parts of a photo along the lines.

5. Edit your photo before you post. There are some amazing apps to help you edit the colors and composition of your photo before you post it. I'm going to list them here and let you go check them out. If it's listed here, I use it. Many of these I'll use together to get the results I want. My best advice is for you to start studying the photos you like as you scroll through your feed and note what you like about each one. What could you do to recreate that look? Here is a list of my favorite photo editing apps:

**PicTapGo** — www.pictapgo.com

**Color Story** — www.acolorstory.com

**PS Express** — www.photoshop.com/products/photoshopexpress

**Mextures** — www.mextures.com

**LensLight** — www.brainfevermedia.com/lenslight.html

**VSCO** — www.vsco.co

**Snapseed** — www.plus.google.com/+Snapseed

**Lightroom** — www.adobe.com/products/lightroom-mobile.html

**WordSwag** — www.wordswag.co

## Videos

I'm not going to get crazy detailed on how to create videos because there are so many platforms that support video now. Videos are such a great way to give your followers a little piece of your real life because they can't really be edited. They can see what you really look like and what your environment is like. I love hearing the people I follow talk to me. I am loving Facebook Live and Instagram Stories for video right now. Snapchat is also a great platform for quick bursts of video about what you're doing. Here are a few tips on how to present videos so people will make it all the way through them.

1. Keep them short. If you're teaching on something, let people know the date and time of the longer class-style video so they know to prepare some time to watch it. Otherwise, two minutes or less.

2. Be succinct. Make sure you're not rambling on. Give them the goods and get out. If you start going in circles, people are going to start tuning out.

3. Give people a good look into your real life or the behind the scenes of your everyday. That keeps people connected to you and gives them some new content to get excited about.

4. Make sure your videos are well lit. Stand facing the window or next to a light source so your viewers can actually see your face.

5. Think about giving little step-by-step tutorials on live video for your viewers to see how to use your product. This lets them ask you real

time questions that you can answer live so they feel like they really get to interact with you and know you.

6. Be careful about what you get when you show videos of your kids. One time I did this cute little morning video that my kids were in not knowing you could see my daughter's underwear through about 1/3 of the video. I had to take it down quick because internet freaks, but if I had been more careful I might have caught it during filming.

7. Think about the background noise. In video you're not only going to have to worry about the picture on the camera but also the sound. If someone is doing construction outside of your house, we're going to hear it. If your kids are screaming bloody murder, you as the mom might be able to tune that out, but as viewers, we won't.

8. There are a lot of great and inexpensive ways to improve the sound quality of your videos. One such way is by purchasing an external mic for your phone. A quick Amazon search will bring up plenty of twenty to thirty dollar options.

9. Have fun, be goofy, and be your real self on video so people get a better sense of your personality that might not come across in your writing. I love that videos let me know the people I may only know through online platforms.

# 8
# EMBRACE CHANGE

## PART EIGHT:

# Embrace Change

It's super important to keep in mind how much change social media is wrapped up in. Change is practically Social Media's middle name. At times, you'll be on a roll. You'll feel like you finally have your favorite platform all figured out, and then they'll go throw a wrench in the program to try to improve their bottom line. They're a business after all and they need to make money just like we do. What you can't do is throw a pity part of one and let it

*when things change*

y o u    h a v e    t o

# ADAPT

derail you. You have to figure out what to do next and you need to do it fast because your competition is already all over it. There's no use crying over it and freaking out. When things change you have to adapt. Find new ways to get the same information in front of your people. Study the analytics. Figure out what makes that platform tick in the new format. Find out how you can make the most of it before the competition does.

Something else you'll need is to embrace new platforms. Don't put off learning what the younger generation is getting into because you never know when you might need it. I hear people tell me all the time, "I don't do Instagram." That's fine if you're just using Facebook for your private social account, but it's just not fine if you're a business trying to get noticed. You have to figure out the platforms where the people are and Instagram has the people. Be willing to try and decide if it's good for your business. Periscope was that for me. I gave it a good try and I actually had a lot of good success and business growth from Periscope, but the amount of random freaks asking to see my feet and talking sexually to me was enough to make me want to quit the internet. It just wasn't worth it for me and thankfully Facebook shot back with Facebook Live and all was right in the world again. Be willing to try what's new and see if you can't make it work for your business. You never know what will be the next big thing.

Outside of platform changes, I want you to think long and hard about the changes your life and the lives of your family are about to go through. Visualize the amazing parts of that change. See that car being paid off, and think of your kids in the private school you want to send them to, visualize the freedom to say all the yes. When I first started my business I knew in my heart of hearts that it was going to be successful and that I would be able to make my family's dreams come true if I tried hard enough. At one point in our lives, Michael and I had to sell a home we bought together for less than we bought it for. We actually had a payment due every month for a house we no longer owned so we could get right-side-up on that debt. On that day, we shook hands and agreed that we would never buy a home again until we could pay for it in cash money.

My start-up business funded that perfect, beautiful, everything-we-wanted-it-to-be home for us this year. We were able to stroke a check for it just like we dreamed we would. I call it my Barbie Dream House and when I look at every piece of that house that will be the home my kids grow up in, I feel like I could burst with pride.

This is the kind of change we're working for, right?

This is the kind of thing we want to be a part of.

This is what we want our kids to see when they think of us.

It's up to you to name it. We are strong, hardworking, capable women who can handle a business and be a great mother at the same time, flaws and all. We're doing the best we can with what we have. Don't forget the kind of change you want in your life. Keep it close so that when the hard parts of entrepreneurship rear their ugly head, you know why you're going to endure it. You remember why you're doing what you do. Work hard, ladies. Make the life you want happen. You have it in you.

# Acknowledgments

One thing you should know about me is that I'm terrible at expressing verbal emotion to others, I feel really stupid when I do (therapy, coming to a Teague Moreno house near you). It's a deep, deep personality flaw. It is therefore imperative that I take the time to list the people who helped me get to the publishing of this book. I would like to thank the following people:

God (is it weird to pray in a book? I'm just going with it): Even though I don't understand all the circumstances, I'm truly grateful for the really hard stuff where I realize you were teaching me the value of grit. There really is beauty in the ashes. Thank you for instilling in me a desire to always want more and opening this door for me to pursue it. High five, Big Guy, see you one day soon.

Michael Moreno: Thanks for keeping things organized and keeping me grounded. I've been a little behind on the laundry and the cleaning and getting the girls ready for school and getting the groceries from the store in the past few years. Worst wife ever. Thank you for loving me anyway. I love you, please don't leave me!

My Lemon Droppers: Thank you for being exactly who you are and nothing more. Thank you for allowing me to be the same. Do we not have the most fun at any job in the history of life? You have inspired me to think bigger, do more and love harder than I ever have in my life. Thanks for understanding the live videos with no shower and no makeup.

Elizabeth Bienas: If I didn't have you to read my mind, I'd surely have lost it about two and a half years ago. Thank you for the ridiculous hours of your day you spend thinking about LTM and the Lemon Droppers and all the other business I somehow find. You always get the job done. Thank you.

The Book Review Board: Thanks for answering all of my questions and reading all the terrible drafts of this book. Mostly, thanks for believing I could do this. I just like you guys.

Mike Salisbury: In January you talked to a girl that had no clue how to do what we just did and for some reason you said yes to that. Thank you for walking me through this entire process and believing in a market for momtrepreneurs.

Jon Acuff: Thanks for being a great connector and for inspiring me. Your gift is in the mail. Spoiler alert: it's a new puppy!

Kelly Anderson-Block: Thanks for having twins along side me and being my closest friend. You always understand when I've just had enough. You and wine keep me sane.

Jen Lake: Thanks for coming in and taking on this project. I am so glad this job was even a possibility for you. I'm so lucky that you know all the things and can fix all the things. Thanks for making me look like I know what I'm doing, I owe you a big case of Dr. Pepper.

Boston, Teagan, & Kennedy: You have perhaps sacrificed the most for this project; time. One day you'll probably need to talk to a counselor about it. You should know, having you is the hardest and the best job I've ever had, and I wouldn't trade it. You're my favorites. Thanks for giving me the time to give to other mommas.